Pathway to Interview success for Project Managers/Agile Project Managers

140 Interview Questions and Answers

Emily Berencroft – Davies

Welcome to 'Pathway to Interview Success for Project Managers/Agile Project Managers: 100 Interview Questions and Answers.' In the dynamic landscape of project management, mastering the art of effective interviews is paramount. Whether you're a seasoned professional or a newcomer to the field, this comprehensive guide is your indispensable companion.

Inside, you'll find a curated selection of 100 meticulously crafted questions and detailed answers designed to challenge, inspire, and empower project and Agile project managers. Each question is meticulously chosen to cover a wide range of topics, from traditional project management methodologies to the latest Agile practices, ensuring that you're thoroughly prepared for any interview scenario.

Whether you're aiming for that coveted promotion, transitioning to a new role, or seeking your dream job, this guide equips you with the knowledge and confidence to excel in your interviews. With practical insights, expert advice, and real-world examples, you'll gain invaluable insights into the intricacies of project management, Agile principles, and effective leadership.

Prepare to elevate your interview performance, impress prospective employers, and take your career to new heights with this book. Let's embark on this journey together and unlock the doors to your professional success."

1. **Question: How does the role of a project manager differ in traditional project management versus Agile project management?**

   Answer: In traditional project management, the project manager typically plays a central role in planning, organizing, and controlling all aspects of the project, often following a predefined plan and focusing on adherence to schedule, budget, and scope. In Agile project management, the role of the project manager shifts to that of a facilitator, coach, and servant-leader, empowering self-organizing teams to collaborate effectively, make decisions, and deliver value incrementally. The Agile project manager focuses on removing obstacles, facilitating communication, and enabling the team to achieve its goals, rather than dictating tasks or imposing rigid processes.

2. **Question: Can you discuss your experience with project risk identification and mitigation?**

   Answer: Certainly. In my previous role, I conducted thorough risk assessments at the beginning of each project, identifying potential risks related to resources, timelines, and stakeholder expectations. I then developed comprehensive risk mitigation plans, which included proactive measures to address risks and contingency plans to manage unforeseen events. Throughout the project, I regularly monitored risks and adjusted mitigation strategies as needed to ensure successful project delivery.

3. **Question: How do you handle project delays or setbacks?**

   Answer: When faced with project delays or setbacks, I first assess the root causes of the issue and communicate transparently with stakeholders about the impact on project timelines and objectives. I then work with the project team to develop a recovery plan, which may involve reallocating resources, adjusting schedules, or renegotiating priorities. Throughout the process, I maintain open communication and provide regular updates to stakeholders to manage expectations and minimize further disruptions.

4. **Question: Can you discuss your experience with project budget management?**

Answer: In my previous roles, I have been responsible for developing and managing project budgets, ensuring that financial resources are allocated effectively to support project objectives. This involves creating detailed budget plans, tracking expenses, and monitoring financial performance throughout the project lifecycle. I also collaborate with finance and accounting teams to ensure compliance with budgetary constraints and address any financial discrepancies or variances proactively.

5. **Question: How do you ensure effective communication within a project team?**

Answer: Effective communication is essential for project success. To ensure clear and open communication within the project team, I establish regular communication channels such as team meetings, status updates, and collaboration tools. I also encourage an open-door policy where team members feel comfortable sharing ideas, concerns, and feedback. Additionally, I provide regular updates on project progress and milestones to keep everyone informed and aligned with project goals.

6. **Question: Can you discuss your experience with project scheduling and timeline management?**

Answer: Yes, I have extensive experience with project scheduling and timeline management. This includes creating detailed project schedules, identifying critical milestones, and allocating resources to meet project deadlines. I use project management software to develop Gantt charts, track progress, and identify dependencies to ensure that projects stay on schedule. I also regularly review and update project schedules to adapt to changing requirements or unforeseen circumstances.

7. **Question: How do you handle project scope creep?**

Answer: Scope creep is a common challenge in project management, and I address it by clearly defining project scope and objectives upfront and establishing a change management process to evaluate and approve any scope changes. I also communicate proactively with stakeholders to manage expectations and prioritize project requirements based on their impact on project goals and timelines. Additionally, I document any scope changes and their implications on project deliverables, resources, and budget to ensure transparency and accountability.

8. **Question: Can you discuss your experience with stakeholder management?**

Answer: Stakeholder management is critical for project success, and I have extensive experience working with stakeholders at various levels to understand their needs, expectations, and concerns. This involves conducting stakeholder analysis, identifying key stakeholders, and developing tailored communication and engagement plans to keep them informed and engaged throughout the project lifecycle. I also address stakeholders' feedback and concerns proactively, seeking their input and buy-in to ensure alignment with project goals and objectives.

9. **Question: How do you handle project risks and issues?**

10. **Answer:** I adopt a proactive approach to project risk management, which involves identifying, assessing, and mitigating risks throughout the project lifecycle. This includes conducting risk assessments, developing risk registers, and implementing risk mitigation strategies to address potential threats to project success. I also establish contingency plans to manage unforeseen events and monitor risks closely to minimize their impact on project objectives. When issues arise, I prioritize them based on their severity and impact on project goals and work with the project team to develop and implement corrective actions to address them promptly.

11. **Question: Can you discuss your experience with project quality management?**

Answer: Quality management is essential for delivering successful projects, and I have extensive experience implementing quality assurance and control processes to ensure project deliverables meet stakeholders' expectations and requirements. This includes defining quality standards, conducting quality reviews and inspections, and implementing quality assurance measures to prevent defects and errors. I also establish quality metrics and performance indicators to measure and monitor project quality throughout the project lifecycle and take corrective actions as needed to address any deviations from quality standards.

12. **Question: How do you handle changes in project requirements?**

Answer: Changes in project requirements are inevitable, and I address them by following a formal change management process to evaluate, approve, and implement changes effectively. This involves assessing the impact of changes on project scope, timeline, and budget, and communicating transparently with stakeholders about the implications of proposed changes. I also work collaboratively with the project team to prioritize requirements based on their impact on project goals and objectives and adjust project plans and schedules accordingly to accommodate approved changes.

13. **Question: Can you discuss your experience with project resource management?**

Answer: Resource management is critical for optimizing project performance, and I have extensive experience managing project resources, including human resources, materials, and equipment. This involves identifying resource requirements, allocating resources effectively to support project objectives, and tracking resource utilization throughout the project lifecycle. I also work closely with resource managers and team leads to ensure that resources are available as needed and address any resource constraints or shortages proactively to minimize their impact on project delivery.

14. **Question: How do you ensure effective collaboration and teamwork within a project team?**

Answer: Effective collaboration and teamwork are essential for project success, and I foster a collaborative work environment by promoting open communication, trust, and respect among team members. This includes establishing clear roles and responsibilities, setting shared goals and objectives, and creating opportunities for team members to collaborate and share knowledge and expertise. I also provide regular feedback and recognition to team members to acknowledge their contributions and encourage a positive and supportive team culture.

15. **Question: Can you discuss your experience with project risk management?**

Answer: Risk management is critical for identifying and mitigating potential threats to project success, and I have extensive experience implementing risk management processes and techniques to manage project risks effectively. This includes conducting risk assessments, identifying and analysing project risks, and developing risk mitigation plans to address potential threats. I also establish risk registers to track and monitor project risks throughout the project lifecycle and take proactive measures to prevent or minimize their impact on project objectives.

16. **Question: How do you handle project changes and updates?**

Answer: I address project changes and updates by following a formal change management process to evaluate, approve, and implement changes effectively. This involves assessing the impact of changes on project scope, timeline, and budget, and communicating transparently with stakeholders about the implications of proposed changes. I also work collaboratively with the project team to prioritize changes based on their impact on project goals and objectives and adjust project plans and schedules accordingly to accommodate approved changes.

17. **Question: Can you discuss your experience with project communication and stakeholder management?**

Answer: Effective communication and stakeholder management are critical for project success, and I have extensive experience developing communication plans and engaging with stakeholders at all levels to ensure alignment with project goals and objectives. This includes conducting stakeholder analysis, identifying key stakeholders, and establishing regular communication channels to keep them informed and engaged throughout the project lifecycle. I also address stakeholders' feedback and concerns proactively, seeking their input and buy-in to ensure project success.

18. **Question: How do you ensure project deliverables meet quality standards?**

Answer: I ensure project deliverables meet quality standards by establishing clear quality criteria and requirements upfront, conducting quality reviews and inspections throughout the project lifecycle, and implementing quality assurance measures to prevent defects and errors.

This includes defining quality metrics and performance indicators to measure and monitor project quality, conducting regular quality audits, and taking corrective actions as needed to address any deviations from quality standards.

19. **Question: Can you discuss your experience with project planning and scheduling?**

Answer: Project planning and scheduling are critical for project success, and I have extensive experience developing detailed project plans and schedules to guide project execution. This includes defining project scope, objectives, and deliverables, identifying project tasks and milestones, and estimating resource requirements and timelines. I also use project management software to create Gantt charts, track progress, and identify dependencies to ensure that projects stay on schedule. I also regularly review and update project plans and schedules to adapt to changing requirements or unforeseen circumstances.

20. **Question: How do you manage project risks and issues?**

Answer: I manage project risks and issues by following a systematic approach to identify, assess, and mitigate risks throughout the project lifecycle. This includes conducting risk assessments, developing risk registers, and implementing risk mitigation strategies to address potential threats to project success. I also establish contingency plans to manage unforeseen events and monitor risks closely to minimize their impact on project objectives. When issues arise, I prioritize them based on their severity and impact on project goals and work with the project team to develop and implement corrective actions to address them promptly.

21. **Question: Can you discuss your experience with project budget management?**

Answer: In my previous roles, I have been responsible for developing and managing project budgets, ensuring that financial resources are allocated effectively to support project objectives. This includes creating detailed budget plans, tracking expenses, and monitoring financial performance throughout the project lifecycle. I also collaborate with finance and accounting teams to ensure compliance with budgetary constraints and address any financial discrepancies or variances proactively.

22. **Question: What is Agile project management, and how does it differ from traditional project management?**

Answer: Agile project management is an iterative approach to managing projects that focuses on delivering value to customers through continuous collaboration, flexibility, and adaptability. Unlike traditional project management, which follows a linear, sequential process, Agile project management emphasizes iterative development, customer feedback, and rapid adaptation to changing requirements and priorities.

23. **Question: Can you discuss your experience with Agile methodologies such as Scrum, Kanban, or XP?**

Answer: I have extensive experience with Agile methodologies such as Scrum, Kanban, and XP, having used them to manage projects in various industries. This includes facilitating Scrum ceremonies such as sprint planning, daily stand-ups, sprint reviews, and retrospectives, implementing Kanban boards to visualize workflow and manage work in progress, and practicing XP principles such as pair programming, test-driven development, and continuous integration.

24. **Question: How do you prioritize the backlog in Agile project management?**

Answer: Prioritizing the backlog in Agile project management involves collaborating with stakeholders to identify and prioritize user stories based on value, effort, and dependencies. This includes conducting backlog grooming sessions to refine user stories, estimate effort, and prioritize them based on business value and project objectives. I also use techniques such as MoSCoW prioritization, story mapping, and relative estimation to prioritize backlog items effectively.

25. **Question: Can you discuss your experience with Agile project estimation and planning?**

Answer: I have extensive experience with Agile project estimation and planning, using techniques such as story points, planning poker, and velocity tracking to estimate effort and plan project iterations. This includes breaking down project requirements into user stories, estimating their complexity and effort, and creating release plans and sprint backlogs to guide project execution. I also use retrospective meetings to review and improve estimation accuracy and planning effectiveness.

26. **Question:** How do you manage project risks and dependencies in Agile project management?

Answer: Managing project risks and dependencies in Agile project management involves identifying, assessing, and mitigating risks throughout the project lifecycle. This includes conducting risk assessments, creating risk registers, and implementing risk mitigation strategies to address potential threats to project success. I also track dependencies between user stories and epics, and collaborate with cross-functional teams to manage dependencies effectively and minimize their impact on project delivery.

27. **Question:** Can you discuss your experience with Agile project retrospectives?

Answer: Certainly. Agile project retrospectives are essential for fostering continuous improvement and enhancing team performance. As an Agile Project Manager, I facilitate retrospectives at the end of each iteration to reflect on what went well, what didn't, and how we can improve. During retrospectives, I create a safe and open environment for team members to share feedback and ideas openly, without fear of judgment. We identify actionable improvements and prioritize them based on their potential impact on team collaboration, communication, and productivity. We then implement changes iteratively, evaluate their effectiveness, and adjust our processes accordingly to enhance team performance and project outcomes.

28. **Question:** How do you ensure effective communication within distributed project teams?

Answer: Effective communication within distributed project teams requires leveraging collaboration tools like video conferencing, instant messaging, and project management software. We establish clear communication channels, hold regular virtual meetings, and provide frequent updates to ensure alignment and transparency. Additionally, we promote a culture of open communication, encourage active participation, and address language and cultural barriers to foster inclusivity and collaboration across geographically dispersed teams.

29. **Question: Can you discuss your experience with project risk identification and mitigation?**

Answer: Identifying and mitigating project risks is crucial for successful project delivery. We conduct thorough risk assessments, involving stakeholders from various departments, to identify potential threats and opportunities. Once risks are identified, we prioritize them based on their impact and likelihood, develop risk mitigation strategies, and assign owners to monitor and manage each risk throughout the project lifecycle. Regular risk reviews and updates ensure proactive risk management, allowing us to address emerging risks promptly and minimize their impact on project objectives.

30. **Question: How do you manage project dependencies and ensure timely delivery?**

Answer: Managing project dependencies involves identifying interdependencies between tasks, activities, and deliverables and coordinating efforts across teams to ensure alignment and synchronization. We create dependency maps, track dependencies closely, and communicate dependencies transparently with stakeholders to facilitate collaboration and mitigate risks. Additionally, we establish clear dependencies within project plans, establish contingency plans for critical dependencies, and regularly review and update dependency logs to ensure timely delivery and minimize disruptions.

31. **Question: Can you discuss your experience with project portfolio management?**

Answer: Project portfolio management involves aligning project investments with organizational goals and strategic objectives. As a Project Manager, I collaborate with senior leadership and stakeholders to define project priorities, assess resource availability, and allocate resources effectively across projects. We use portfolio management tools and techniques to evaluate project portfolios, balance risks and rewards, and optimize resource utilization to maximize value and achieve organizational objectives. Regular portfolio reviews and governance ensure transparency, accountability, and alignment with business priorities.

32. **Question: How do you foster a culture of continuous improvement within project teams?**

Answer: Fostering a culture of continuous improvement involves encouraging team members to seek feedback, reflect on their experiences, and identify opportunities for growth and development. We conduct regular retrospectives to reflect on project performance, celebrate successes, and identify areas for improvement. Additionally, we encourage knowledge sharing, provide opportunities for skill development, and recognize and reward innovation and initiative to motivate team members and foster a culture of continuous learning and improvement.

33. **Question: Can you discuss your experience with Agile project management frameworks other than Scrum, such as Lean or Extreme Programming (XP)?**

Answer: Agile project management encompasses various frameworks and methodologies, each with its unique principles and practices. For example, Lean focuses on eliminating waste and maximizing value delivery by streamlining processes and optimizing workflow. Extreme Programming (XP) emphasizes technical excellence, collaboration, and customer feedback through practices like pair programming, test-driven development, and continuous integration. In my experience, I've applied Lean principles to identify and eliminate inefficiencies in project processes and leverage XP practices to enhance product quality and customer satisfaction.

34. **Question: How do you ensure alignment between project goals and organizational objectives?**

Answer: Ensuring alignment between project goals and organizational objectives requires understanding the strategic priorities and business needs of the organization. As a Project Manager, I collaborate closely with stakeholders at all levels to define project objectives, clarify expectations, and establish key performance indicators (KPIs) to measure project success. We conduct regular check-ins with senior leadership to review project progress, address concerns, and realign priorities as needed to ensure that projects deliver value and contribute to the achievement of organizational goals.

35. **Question:** Can you discuss your experience with change management in project management?

Answer: Change management is essential for navigating project complexities and addressing evolving stakeholder needs and requirements. We establish change control processes to evaluate and approve proposed changes, assess their impact on project scope, timeline, and budget, and communicate changes transparently with stakeholders. We also conduct stakeholder engagement activities to manage resistance to change, build support for proposed changes, and ensure smooth transitions throughout the project lifecycle. Regular change reviews and updates help us adapt to changing circumstances and minimize disruptions to project delivery.

36. **Question:** How do you ensure that project deliverables meet quality standards and customer expectations?

Answer: Ensuring that project deliverables meet quality standards and customer expectations requires implementing robust quality assurance and control processes. We define quality criteria and acceptance criteria upfront, conduct regular quality reviews and inspections throughout the project lifecycle, and engage stakeholders in user acceptance testing to validate deliverables against agreed-upon requirements. We also leverage quality management tools and techniques to identify defects and non-conformities, implement corrective actions, and continuously improve product quality and customer satisfaction.

37. **Question:** Can you discuss your experience with stakeholder engagement and communication?

Answer: Stakeholder engagement and communication are critical for project success, and I prioritize building and maintaining positive relationships with stakeholders at all levels. This involves conducting stakeholder analysis to identify key stakeholders, understand their interests and concerns, and tailor communication strategies to meet their needs. We establish regular communication channels, hold stakeholder meetings and workshops, and provide timely updates and progress reports to keep stakeholders informed and engaged throughout the project lifecycle. We also solicit feedback, address concerns, and seek buy-in from stakeholders to ensure alignment with project goals and objectives.

38. **Question: How do you handle project scope changes or scope creep?**

Answer: Handling project scope changes or scope creep involves evaluating proposed changes, assessing their impact on project objectives, and communicating transparently with stakeholders about the implications of changes. We follow a formal change control process to document and review change requests, prioritize them based on their value and alignment with project goals, and obtain approval from the project sponsor or change control board before implementing changes. We also conduct impact assessments to identify any downstream effects on project scope, timeline, or budget and adjust plans accordingly to minimize disruptions and ensure project success.

39. **Question: Can you discuss your experience with resource allocation and capacity planning in project management?**

Answer: Resource allocation and capacity planning are critical for optimizing resource utilization and ensuring project success. As a Project Manager, I collaborate with resource managers and team leads to identify resource requirements, allocate resources effectively to support project objectives, and track resource utilization throughout the project lifecycle. We leverage resource management tools and techniques to forecast resource demand, identify resource constraints or shortages, and adjust plans as needed to balance workload and optimize resource utilization. Regular capacity planning reviews and updates help us anticipate resource needs and proactively address any staffing issues or bottlenecks to minimize risks and ensure timely project delivery.

40. **Question: How do you ensure that projects are delivered on time and within budget?**

Answer: Delivering projects on time and within budget requires careful planning, monitoring, and control throughout the project lifecycle. We develop detailed project plans and schedules, identify critical milestones and dependencies, and allocate resources effectively to support project objectives. We track project progress and performance against baseline estimates, identify deviations from planned targets, and implement corrective actions to address schedule or budget variances proactively. Regular project reviews and updates help us identify and mitigate risks, optimize resource utilization, and ensure that projects stay on track to meet delivery deadlines and financial targets.

41. **Question:** Can you discuss your experience with project governance and compliance?

Answer: Project governance and compliance are essential for ensuring that projects are executed in alignment with organizational policies, regulations, and industry standards. As a Project Manager, I establish project governance frameworks, define roles and responsibilities, and implement project management methodologies and best practices to guide project execution and ensure compliance with internal and external requirements. We conduct regular project audits and assessments to monitor project performance, identify any deviations from governance standards, and implement corrective actions to address compliance issues promptly. We also engage stakeholders and subject matter experts to provide guidance and support on governance matters and promote a culture of transparency, accountability, and integrity throughout the project lifecycle.

42. **Question:** How do you facilitate collaboration and communication within Agile project teams?

Answer: Facilitating collaboration and communication within Agile project teams is essential for driving productivity and delivering value to customers. We use various techniques and tools such as daily stand-up meetings, Kanban boards, and collaborative software platforms to ensure that team members stay aligned, share information, and coordinate efforts effectively. We also encourage open and transparent communication, foster a culture of trust and respect, and provide opportunities for team members to voice their ideas, concerns, and feedback freely. Additionally, we conduct regular team-building activities and workshops to strengthen relationships, build camaraderie, and enhance collaboration within the team.

43. **Question: How do you measure and track team performance in Agile project management?**

Answer: Measuring and tracking team performance in Agile project management involves using key performance indicators (KPIs) and metrics to assess progress, identify areas for improvement, and optimize team effectiveness. We track metrics such as sprint velocity, cycle time, and burn-down charts to monitor progress, identify bottlenecks, and adjust plans accordingly. We also conduct regular retrospectives to reflect on team performance, celebrate successes, and identify opportunities for growth and development. Additionally, we solicit feedback from stakeholders and customers to evaluate the quality of deliverables, satisfaction with the process, and overall project performance.

44. **Question: How do you manage conflicts and resolve disagreements within Agile project teams?**

Answer: Managing conflicts and resolving disagreements within Agile project teams requires effective communication, active listening, and conflict resolution skills. We create a safe and supportive team environment where team members feel comfortable expressing their opinions, concerns, and feedback openly. We encourage constructive dialogue and collaboration, facilitate discussions to identify root causes of conflicts, and work together to find mutually acceptable solutions. We also establish ground rules and norms for team interactions, address conflicts promptly, and escalate unresolved issues to higher levels of management if necessary.

45. **Question: Can you discuss your experience with Agile project retrospectives?**

Answer: Agile project retrospectives are essential for promoting continuous improvement and enhancing team performance. As an Agile Project Manager, I facilitate retrospectives at the end of each iteration to reflect on what went well, what didn't, and how we can improve. During retrospectives, I create a safe and open environment for team members to share feedback and ideas openly, without fear of judgment. We identify actionable improvements, prioritize them based on their potential impact, and implement changes to enhance team collaboration, communication, and productivity. We also conduct regular retrospectives to review and improve our processes iteratively, ensuring that we deliver high-quality products that meet customer needs effectively.

46. **Question:** How do you handle project scope changes or new requirements in Agile project management?

Answer: Handling project scope changes or new requirements in Agile project management requires flexibility, adaptability, and collaboration. We follow a formal change management process to evaluate and prioritize proposed changes, assess their impact on project objectives, and communicate transparently with stakeholders about the implications of changes. We engage with the product owner and stakeholders to understand the rationale behind the changes, negotiate trade-offs, and make informed decisions about whether to accept, reject, or defer the changes. We also update the product backlog and sprint backlog accordingly, adjust project plans and schedules as needed, and ensure that the team remains focused on delivering value to customers iteratively.

47. **Question:** Can you discuss your experience with Agile project planning and estimation?

Answer: Agile project planning and estimation involve breaking down project requirements into user stories, estimating effort, and creating release plans and sprint backlogs to guide project execution. As an Agile Project Manager, I collaborate with the product owner and development team to define user stories, prioritize backlog items, and estimate effort collaboratively. We use techniques like story points, planning poker, and relative estimation to estimate the complexity and effort of user stories accurately. We then create release plans and sprint backlogs to allocate resources and prioritize work based on project objectives and stakeholder expectations. Throughout the project, we conduct regular planning sessions, adjust plans iteratively, and refine our estimation techniques to improve accuracy and predictability.

48. **Question: How do you ensure that project deliverables meet quality standards in Agile project management?**

Answer: Ensuring that project deliverables meet quality standards in Agile project management requires implementing robust quality assurance and control processes. We define quality criteria and acceptance criteria upfront, conduct regular quality reviews and inspections throughout the project lifecycle, and engage stakeholders in user acceptance testing to validate deliverables against agreed-upon requirements. We leverage automated testing tools and techniques to identify defects and non-conformities early in the development process, address them promptly, and ensure that the product meets quality standards and customer expectations. We also conduct regular retrospectives to reflect on our quality management practices, identify opportunities for improvement, and implement changes to enhance product quality and customer satisfaction.

49. **Question: Can you discuss your experience with Agile project risk management?**

Answer: Agile project risk management involves identifying, assessing, and mitigating risks throughout the project lifecycle. As an Agile Project Manager, I collaborate with the development team, product owner, and stakeholders to identify potential risks, analyze their impact and likelihood, and develop risk mitigation strategies to address them effectively. We create risk registers to track and monitor risks, assign owners to manage each risk, and implement proactive measures to prevent or minimize their impact on project objectives. We also conduct regular risk reviews and updates, adjust risk management strategies as needed, and communicate risk status transparently with stakeholders to ensure that they are informed and engaged in risk management activities.

50. **Question: How do you prioritize work and manage dependencies in Agile project management?**

Answer: Prioritizing work and managing dependencies in Agile project management involves collaborating with the product owner and development team to define user stories, prioritize backlog items, and manage work in progress effectively. We use techniques like MoSCoW prioritization, story mapping, and relative estimation to prioritize backlog items based on business value, urgency, and dependencies. We create dependency maps to visualize and manage dependencies between user stories, epics, and teams, ensuring that cross-functional teams collaborate effectively and deliver value to customers iteratively. We also conduct regular backlog grooming sessions, adjust priorities as needed, and communicate changes transparently with stakeholders to ensure alignment and minimize risks.

51. **Question: Can you discuss your experience with Agile project documentation and knowledge sharing?**

Answer: Agile project documentation and knowledge sharing are essential for capturing project artifacts, sharing information, and facilitating collaboration within project teams. As an Agile Project Manager, I ensure that project documentation is lightweight, accessible, and up-to-date, reflecting the current state of the project and supporting team collaboration and decision-making. We use tools like wikis, document repositories, and collaboration platforms to document project requirements, user stories, design decisions, and technical specifications, making them accessible to all team members and stakeholders. We also promote knowledge sharing through regular team meetings, workshops, and training sessions, encouraging team members to share their expertise, lessons learned, and best practices to enhance team productivity and project outcomes.

52. **Question: How do you ensure that Agile ceremonies, such as sprint planning and daily stand-ups, are effective?**

Answer: Ensuring the effectiveness of Agile ceremonies involves setting clear objectives, establishing ground rules, and fostering active participation and collaboration among team members. During sprint planning, we define sprint goals, prioritize backlog items, and estimate effort collaboratively to ensure that the team understands the scope and expectations for the upcoming sprint. During daily stand-ups, we focus on sharing progress, identifying impediments, and coordinating efforts to keep the team aligned and focused on sprint goals. We encourage open and transparent communication, address any blockers or concerns promptly, and follow up on action items to ensure that the team stays on track and delivers value to customers consistently.

53. **Question: How do you handle changes to project scope or requirements during an Agile project?**

Answer: Handling changes to project scope or requirements during an Agile project involves following a formal change management process to evaluate, prioritize, and implement changes effectively. We collaborate with the product owner and stakeholders to assess the impact of proposed changes on project objectives, timeline, and budget, and make informed decisions about whether to accept, reject, or defer the changes. We update the product backlog and sprint backlog accordingly, adjust project plans and schedules as needed, and communicate changes transparently with stakeholders to ensure alignment and minimize risks. We also conduct regular backlog grooming sessions to review and refine backlog items, address any emerging requirements, and adapt our plans iteratively to deliver value to customers.

54. **Question: How do you ensure that Agile teams remain motivated and engaged throughout the project?**

Answer: Ensuring that Agile teams remain motivated and engaged throughout the project involves creating a supportive team environment, recognizing and celebrating achievements, and providing opportunities for growth and development. We foster a culture of trust, respect, and collaboration, where team members feel empowered to voice their ideas, concerns, and feedback openly. We recognize and reward individual and team accomplishments, celebrate milestones and successes, and provide constructive feedback and coaching to help team members grow and develop their skills. We also promote work-life balance, encourage self-care, and provide resources and support to help team members manage stress and burnout effectively.

55. **Question: How do you manage stakeholder expectations and ensure alignment with project goals?**

Answer: Managing stakeholder expectations and ensuring alignment with project goals involves establishing clear communication channels, managing relationships proactively, and engaging stakeholders throughout the project lifecycle. We conduct stakeholder analysis to identify key stakeholders, understand their needs and expectations, and develop tailored communication and engagement plans to keep them informed and engaged. We establish regular communication channels, hold stakeholder meetings and workshops, and provide timely updates and progress reports to address any concerns or issues proactively. We also seek feedback from stakeholders regularly, address their concerns and expectations, and adapt our plans and strategies to ensure alignment with project goals and objectives.

56. **Question: How do you ensure that Agile project teams have the necessary resources and support to succeed?**

Answer: Ensuring that Agile project teams have the necessary resources and support to succeed involves collaborating with resource managers and stakeholders to identify resource requirements, allocate resources effectively, and remove any impediments or obstacles that may hinder team progress. We conduct resource planning and capacity assessments to ensure that teams have the right mix of skills and expertise to deliver on project objectives. We provide training and professional development opportunities to help team members enhance their skills and knowledge. We also address any resource constraints or bottlenecks promptly, escalate issues as needed, and advocate for the team to ensure that they have the support and resources they need to succeed.

57. **Question: How do you measure the success of Agile projects and assess their impact on business outcomes?**

Answer: Measuring the success of Agile projects and assessing their impact on business outcomes involves defining key performance indicators (KPIs), collecting relevant metrics and data, and analyzing project performance against predefined targets and benchmarks. We track metrics such as sprint velocity, cycle time, and burn-down charts to monitor progress, identify bottlenecks, and optimize team performance. We also conduct regular reviews and retrospectives to reflect on project performance, celebrate successes, and identify opportunities for improvement. Additionally, we solicit feedback from stakeholders and customers to evaluate the quality of deliverables, satisfaction with the process, and overall project success. By analyzing these metrics and insights, we can assess the impact of Agile projects on business outcomes and make data-driven decisions to drive continuous improvement and value delivery.

58. **Question: How do you ensure that Agile project teams adhere to project timelines and deliverables?**

    Answer: Ensuring that Agile project teams adhere to project timelines and deliverables involves setting clear expectations, establishing accountability, and providing support and guidance as needed. We develop detailed project plans and schedules, identify critical milestones and dependencies, and allocate resources effectively to support project objectives. We conduct regular sprint planning sessions to define sprint goals, prioritize backlog items, and estimate effort collaboratively with the team. We monitor project progress and performance against baseline estimates, identify any deviations from planned targets, and implement corrective actions to address schedule variances proactively. We also conduct regular reviews and retrospectives to reflect on project performance, identify areas for improvement, and make adjustments to our plans and strategies as needed to ensure that we meet project timelines and deliverables effectively.

59. **Question: Describe a project where you had to navigate conflicting priorities from stakeholders. How did you prioritize tasks and manage stakeholder expectations?**

    Answer: In a complex project involving multiple stakeholders with competing interests, I used a strategic approach to prioritize tasks and manage expectations. I conducted stakeholder analysis to understand their priorities and concerns, and I facilitated discussions to find common ground and alignment on project objectives. I also provided regular updates and progress reports to keep stakeholders informed of our progress and address any concerns proactively. By fostering transparent communication and collaboration, we were able to navigate the conflicting priorities and achieve consensus on key project deliverables.

60. **Question: How do you foster a culture of innovation and experimentation within Agile project teams?**

    Answer: Fostering a culture of innovation and experimentation within Agile project teams involves encouraging creativity, embracing failure as a learning opportunity, and providing a supportive environment for experimentation and exploration. We promote a growth mindset, where team members feel empowered to take risks, challenge the status quo, and pursue innovative solutions to complex problems. We provide resources and support to help team members explore new ideas, experiment with different approaches, and learn from their experiences. We also celebrate successes and failures alike, recognizing and rewarding innovation, creativity, and initiative to motivate and inspire team members to push the boundaries and achieve breakthrough results. By fostering a culture of innovation and experimentation, we can drive continuous improvement, drive competitive advantage, and deliver value to customers more effectively.

61. **Question:** How do you prioritize backlog items and manage stakeholder expectations in Agile project management?

Answer: Prioritizing backlog items and managing stakeholder expectations in Agile project management involves collaboration and communication to ensure alignment with project goals and objectives. We work closely with the product owner and stakeholders to define user stories, prioritize backlog items, and manage expectations effectively. We use techniques like MoSCoW prioritization, story mapping, and relative estimation to prioritize backlog items based on business value, urgency, and dependencies. We conduct regular backlog grooming sessions to review and refine backlog items, address any emerging requirements, and adapt our plans iteratively to deliver value to customers. We also communicate transparently with stakeholders, provide timely updates and progress reports, and solicit feedback to ensure alignment and minimize risks.

62. **Question:** How do you manage project dependencies and coordinate efforts across Agile project teams?

Answer: Managing project dependencies and coordinating efforts across Agile project teams requires collaboration, communication, and coordination to ensure alignment and synchronization. We create dependency maps to visualize and manage dependencies between user stories, epics, and teams, ensuring that cross-functional teams collaborate effectively and deliver value to customers iteratively. We establish clear communication channels, hold regular stand-up meetings, and use collaboration tools like Kanban boards and project management software to track progress, identify bottlenecks, and coordinate efforts across teams. We also conduct regular synchronization meetings to review dependencies, address any conflicts or constraints, and adjust plans as needed to ensure that project objectives are met effectively.

63. **Question: How do you ensure that Agile project teams have the necessary skills and expertise to deliver on project objectives?**

    Answer: Ensuring that Agile project teams have the necessary skills and expertise to deliver on project objectives involves identifying training and development needs, providing opportunities for skill enhancement, and promoting knowledge sharing and collaboration within the team. We conduct skills assessments to identify gaps in team capabilities and develop tailored training and development plans to address them. We provide resources and support to help team members acquire new skills and knowledge, such as training programs, workshops, and mentoring opportunities. We also promote knowledge sharing and collaboration within the team, encouraging team members to share their expertise, lessons learned, and best practices to enhance team productivity and project outcomes.

64. **Question: How do you handle changes to project scope or requirements in Agile project management?**

    Answer: Handling changes to project scope or requirements in Agile project management involves following a formal change management process to evaluate, prioritize, and implement changes effectively. We collaborate with the product owner and stakeholders to assess the impact of proposed changes on project objectives, timeline, and budget, and make informed decisions about whether to accept, reject, or defer the changes. We update the product backlog and sprint backlog accordingly, adjust project plans and schedules as needed, and communicate changes transparently with stakeholders to ensure alignment and minimize risks. We also conduct regular backlog grooming sessions to review and refine backlog items, address any emerging requirements, and adapt our plans iteratively to deliver value to customers.

65. **Question:** Describe a project where you had to manage conflicting priorities between different project stakeholders. How did you navigate these conflicts and ensure alignment on project objectives?

Answer: In a project involving multiple stakeholders with conflicting priorities, I facilitated stakeholder workshops to identify common goals and objectives and foster consensus on project priorities. I encouraged stakeholders to voice their concerns and perspectives openly and facilitated constructive dialogue to find mutually acceptable solutions. I also leveraged data and evidence to support decision-making and prioritization, focusing on the project's overarching goals and strategic objectives. By promoting transparency, collaboration, and compromise, we were able to navigate the conflicting priorities and achieve alignment on project objectives.

66. **Question:** How do you measure and track project progress in Agile project management?

Answer: Measuring and tracking project progress in Agile project management involves using key performance indicators (KPIs) and metrics to assess progress, identify bottlenecks, and optimize team performance. We track metrics such as sprint velocity, cycle time, and burn-down charts to monitor progress, identify any deviations from planned targets, and adjust plans accordingly. We also conduct regular sprint reviews and retrospectives to reflect on project performance, celebrate successes, and identify opportunities for improvement. Additionally, we solicit feedback from stakeholders and customers to evaluate the quality of deliverables, satisfaction with the process, and overall project success. By analyzing these metrics and insights, we can assess project progress effectively and make data-driven decisions to drive continuous improvement and value delivery.

67. **Question:** How do you manage project risks and ensure that they are addressed effectively?

Answer: Managing project risks in Agile project management involves identifying, assessing, and mitigating risks throughout the project lifecycle. We collaborate with the development team, product owner, and stakeholders to identify potential risks, analyse their impact and likelihood, and develop risk mitigation strategies to address them effectively. We create risk registers to track and monitor risks, assign owners to manage each risk, and implement proactive measures to prevent or minimize their impact on project objectives. We also conduct regular risk reviews and updates, adjust risk management strategies as needed, and communicate risk status transparently with stakeholders to ensure that they are informed and engaged in risk management activities.

68. **Question: How do you ensure that project deliverables meet quality standards and customer expectations?**

Answer: Ensuring that project deliverables meet quality standards and customer expectations requires implementing robust quality assurance and control processes. We define quality criteria and acceptance criteria upfront, conduct regular quality reviews and inspections throughout the project lifecycle, and engage stakeholders in user acceptance testing to validate deliverables against agreed-upon requirements. We leverage automated testing tools and techniques to identify defects and non-conformities early in the development process, address them promptly, and ensure that the product meets quality standards and customer expectations. We also conduct regular retrospectives to reflect on our quality management practices, identify opportunities for improvement, and implement changes to enhance product quality and customer satisfaction.

69. **Question: How do you ensure that project teams remain aligned with project goals and objectives?**

Answer: Ensuring that project teams remain aligned with project goals and objectives involves setting clear expectations, establishing accountability, and providing support and guidance as needed. We develop a shared understanding of project goals and objectives, define key performance indicators (KPIs) and success criteria, and communicate them to all team members. We hold regular team meetings and checkpoints to review progress, address any concerns or issues, and realign priorities as needed. We also provide ongoing feedback and coaching to help team members stay focused and motivated, celebrate successes, and address any challenges or obstacles that may arise along the way.

70. **Question: How do you manage stakeholder expectations and ensure effective communication?**

Answer: Managing stakeholder expectations and ensuring effective communication involves establishing clear communication channels, managing relationships proactively, and engaging stakeholders throughout the project lifecycle. We conduct stakeholder analysis to identify key stakeholders, understand their needs and expectations, and develop tailored communication and engagement plans to keep them informed and engaged. We establish regular communication channels, hold stakeholder meetings and workshops, and provide timely updates and progress reports to address any concerns or issues proactively. We also seek feedback from stakeholders regularly, address their concerns and expectations, and adapt our plans and strategies to ensure alignment with project goals and objectives.

71. **Question: How do you foster a culture of collaboration and teamwork within project teams?**

Answer: Fostering a culture of collaboration and teamwork within project teams involves creating a supportive team environment, promoting open communication, and encouraging collective ownership and accountability for project success. We establish ground rules and norms for team interactions, such as active listening, respect, and constructive feedback, to ensure that all team members feel valued and included. We promote a growth mindset, where team members feel empowered to take risks, challenge the status quo, and pursue innovative solutions to complex problems. We also provide opportunities for team building and bonding, such as team lunches, off-site retreats, and collaborative workshops, to strengthen relationships, build trust, and enhance collaboration within the team.

72. **Question: How do you handle changes to project scope or requirements during an Agile project?**

Answer: Handling changes to project scope or requirements during an Agile project involves following a formal change management process to evaluate, prioritize, and implement changes effectively. We collaborate with the product owner and stakeholders to assess the impact of proposed changes on project objectives, timeline, and budget, and make informed decisions about whether to accept, reject, or defer the changes. We update the product backlog and sprint backlog accordingly, adjust project plans and schedules as needed, and communicate changes transparently with stakeholders to ensure alignment and minimize risks. We also conduct regular backlog grooming sessions to review and refine backlog items, address any emerging requirements, and adapt our plans iteratively to deliver value to customers.

73. **Question:** Can you recall a project where you had to manage a high-stress situation or crisis? How did you maintain composure and lead the team through the challenging period?

Answer: In a project facing a critical deadline with significant technical issues, I remained calm and composed under pressure to provide leadership and guidance to the team. I conducted regular check-ins with team members to assess their well-being and address any concerns or challenges they were facing. I also communicated transparently with stakeholders about the situation and our mitigation efforts, managing expectations and providing reassurance about our ability to overcome the challenges. By demonstrating resilience and empathy, I was able to maintain team morale and focus during the high-stress period and successfully navigate the project to completion.

74. **Question:** How do you ensure that project teams remain focused on delivering value to customers in Agile project management?
    Answer: Ensuring that project teams remain focused on delivering value to customers in Agile project management involves setting clear expectations, establishing priorities, and aligning efforts with customer needs and requirements. We develop a shared understanding of customer expectations, define key performance indicators (KPIs) and success criteria, and communicate them to all team members. We prioritize backlog items based on business value, urgency, and dependencies, ensuring that the team focuses on delivering the most valuable features and functionality first. We conduct regular sprint reviews and retrospectives to reflect on project performance, celebrate successes, and identify opportunities for improvement. We also solicit feedback from stakeholders and customers regularly, address their concerns and

expectations, and adapt our plans and strategies to ensure alignment with customer needs and expectations.

75. **Question: How do you ensure that Agile project teams adhere to project timelines and deliverables?**

Answer: Ensuring that Agile project teams adhere to project timelines and deliverables involves setting clear expectations, establishing accountability, and providing support and guidance as needed. We develop detailed project plans and schedules, identify critical milestones and dependencies, and allocate resources effectively to support project objectives. We conduct regular sprint planning sessions to define sprint goals, prioritize backlog items, and estimate effort collaboratively with the team. We monitor project progress and performance against baseline estimates, identify any deviations from planned targets, and implement corrective actions to address schedule variances proactively. We also conduct regular reviews and retrospectives to reflect on project performance, identify areas for improvement, and make adjustments to our plans and strategies as needed to ensure that we meet project timelines and deliverables effectively.

76. **Question: How does the concept of "continuous improvement" in Lean UX and Extreme Programming (XP) contribute to Agile project management practices?**

Answer: The concept of "continuous improvement" in Lean UX and Extreme Programming (XP) contributes to Agile project management practices by fostering a culture of learning, adaptation, and innovation. Lean UX encourages teams to iterate rapidly, experiment, and learn from failures to improve their designs and products continuously. By embracing a mindset of continuous improvement, teams can identify areas for optimization, refine their processes, and deliver higher-quality products that better meet user needs and business goals. Similarly, XP promotes a culture of continuous improvement through practices like frequent retrospectives, where teams reflect on their process, identify strengths and weaknesses, and make adjustments to improve their effectiveness and efficiency over time.

77. Question: How does the "Just-In-Time" (JIT) principle in Lean UX and Kanban support Agile principles of minimizing waste and maximizing value delivery?

Answer: The "Just-In-Time" (JIT) principle in Lean UX and Kanban supports Agile principles of minimizing waste and maximizing value delivery by ensuring that work is completed only when it is needed and adding value. JIT eliminates unnecessary waiting time, overproduction, and excess inventory by synchronizing work to customer demand and delivering it just in time to meet that demand. In Lean UX, JIT encourages teams to prioritize work items based on customer feedback and business value, focusing on delivering the most valuable features first. In Kanban, JIT limits work in progress (WIP) to match available capacity, preventing overloading and optimizing flow. By embracing JIT principles, teams can reduce waste, increase efficiency, and deliver value more effectively.

78. Question: Can you describe a project where you faced significant challenges in meeting deadlines? How did you handle the situation?

Answer: In one project, we encountered unexpected delays due to technical issues with a vendor's software. To address this, I convened an emergency meeting with the project team and stakeholders to reassess our timeline and identify potential solutions. We decided to allocate additional resources to resolve the technical issues and implemented a revised project plan with more realistic deadlines. By proactively addressing the challenges and adjusting our approach, we were able to meet the project deadlines without compromising on quality.

79. Question: How does the concept of "flow efficiency" in Kanban contribute to Agile project management practices?

Answer: The concept of "flow efficiency" in Kanban contributes to Agile project management practices by focusing on maximizing the smooth and continuous flow of work through the system. Flow efficiency measures the percentage of time spent actively working on a task versus the total time it takes to complete the task, including waiting time and delays. By optimizing flow efficiency, teams can reduce lead times, minimize bottlenecks, and deliver value more quickly and predictably. This enables teams to respond more effectively to changing priorities and customer needs, ultimately improving overall productivity and customer satisfaction.

80. **Question:** How does the "Definition of Done" in Scrum and the "Definition of Ready" in Kanban ensure that work meets quality standards and is ready for delivery?

   Answer: The "Definition of Done" in Scrum and the "Definition of Ready" in Kanban are both criteria that define when work is considered complete and ready for the next stage of the workflow. The "Definition of Done" typically includes criteria such as code review, testing, documentation, and acceptance criteria, ensuring that work meets quality standards and is ready for release to customers. Similarly, the "Definition of Ready" specifies criteria that work must meet before it can be pulled into the active part of the workflow, such as clear requirements, acceptance criteria, and dependencies resolved. By establishing clear criteria for what constitutes "done" and "ready," teams can maintain consistency, quality, and transparency in their work processes.

81. **Question:** How can teams use metrics such as lead time and cycle time in Kanban to identify opportunities for process improvement and optimize their workflow?

   Answer: Teams can use metrics such as lead time and cycle time in Kanban to identify opportunities for process improvement and optimize their workflow. Lead time measures the total time it takes for a work item to move through the entire workflow, from request to delivery. Cycle time measures the time it takes for a work item to move through the active part of the workflow, from when work begins to when it is completed. By tracking these metrics and analysing trends over time, teams can identify bottlenecks, reduce waste, and make targeted improvements to streamline their process and increase efficiency.

82. **Question:** How does the concept of "pull-based" work management in Kanban align with Agile principles of flexibility and adaptability?

   Answer: The concept of "pull-based" work management in Kanban aligns with Agile principles of flexibility and adaptability by empowering teams to respond quickly to changing priorities and customer needs. In Kanban, work is pulled into the system based on available capacity rather than pushed based on predetermined schedules or deadlines.

This allows teams to focus on completing work as it becomes ready, minimizing waste and maximizing flow. By embracing a pull-based approach, teams can adapt to fluctuations in demand, optimize their workflow, and deliver value more efficiently, all while maintaining a sustainable pace.

83. Question: How do Scrum and Extreme Programming (XP) practices overlap, and how can teams leverage their synergies in Agile software development?

Answer: Scrum and Extreme Programming (XP) practices overlap in their emphasis on iterative development, collaboration, and continuous improvement. Both frameworks promote self-organizing teams, frequent feedback, and delivering value incrementally. Teams can leverage their synergies by combining Scrum's structured framework with XP's technical practices, such as Test-Driven Development (TDD), Pair Programming, and Continuous Integration. By incorporating XP practices into their Scrum workflow, teams can enhance code quality, reduce defects, and increase productivity, leading to faster delivery of high-quality software.

84. Question: Have you ever managed a project where scope creep became a challenge? How did you prevent scope creep and ensure project scope remained manageable?

Answer: Yes, in a previous project, we encountered scope creep due to changing requirements from stakeholders. To address this, I implemented a formal change control process to evaluate and approve any proposed changes to the project scope. I collaborated closely with stakeholders to assess the impact of proposed changes on project objectives, timeline, and budget, and I prioritized changes based on their alignment with project goals. By establishing clear criteria for evaluating scope changes and maintaining stakeholder engagement throughout the process, we were able to prevent scope creep and deliver the project successfully.

85. Question: How can teams apply the principles of Lean UX to enhance user engagement and satisfaction in Agile projects?

Answer: Teams can apply the principles of Lean UX to enhance user engagement and satisfaction in Agile projects by prioritizing user needs, validating assumptions through experimentation, and delivering value early and often. Lean UX encourages teams to focus on outcomes over outputs, meaning they prioritize solving user problems and delivering meaningful experiences rather than just shipping features. By incorporating user feedback into the design process and iterating based on real-world usage, teams can create products that are more intuitive, useful, and delightful for users.

86.**Question: How do Scrum, Kanban, Lean UX, and Extreme Programming (XP) promote cross-functional collaboration within Agile teams?**

Answer: Scrum, Kanban, Lean UX, and Extreme Programming (XP) promote cross-functional collaboration within Agile teams by encouraging diverse perspectives, shared ownership, and collective responsibility for delivering value. Scrum emphasizes self-organizing teams with a shared commitment to achieving sprint goals. Kanban encourages collaboration through visual management and limiting work in progress. Lean UX fosters collaboration between designers, developers, and stakeholders through co-creation and rapid iteration. XP promotes collaboration through practices like Pair Programming and Collective Code Ownership, where team members work together closely to solve problems and share knowledge.

87.**Question: In what ways can Extreme Programming (XP) practices be integrated with Scrum and Kanban methodologies to enhance software development?**

Answer: Extreme Programming (XP) practices can be integrated with Scrum and Kanban methodologies to enhance software development by promoting technical excellence, collaboration, and continuous improvement. Practices such as Test-Driven Development (TDD), Pair Programming, and Continuous Integration can complement Scrum and Kanban by ensuring code quality, reducing defects, and increasing team productivity. By incorporating XP practices into their workflows, teams can deliver high-quality software more efficiently, adapt to changing requirements, and foster a culture of shared responsibility and ownership.

88.**Question: How does Lean UX integrate with Scrum and Kanban to enhance user-centric design in Agile projects?**

Answer: Lean UX integrates with Scrum and Kanban by emphasizing collaboration, experimentation, and rapid feedback loops throughout the design and development process. Teams can use Lean UX principles to align user needs with business goals, prioritize features based on value, and iterate quickly based on user feedback. By incorporating Lean UX practices into Scrum and Kanban workflows, teams can deliver user-centric products more effectively, reduce waste, and increase customer satisfaction.

89.**Question:** How can Scrum and Kanban complement each other in Agile project management?

Answer: Scrum and Kanban can complement each other by combining Scrum's structured framework with Kanban's flexibility and continuous flow approach. Teams can use Scrum for sprint planning, sprint reviews, and retrospectives to establish cadence and deliver value iteratively, while leveraging Kanban for visualizing work, limiting work in progress, and optimizing flow between sprints. This combination allows teams to maintain agility, respond to changing priorities, and continuously improve their process.

90.**Question:** What is Kanban, and how does it differ from Scrum?

Answer: Kanban is an Agile methodology focused on visualizing work, limiting work in progress (WIP), and optimizing flow. Unlike Scrum, which operates in fixed-length sprints with predefined roles and ceremonies, Kanban is more flexible and continuous. It allows teams to visualize their workflow on a Kanban board, with columns representing different stages of the process, from backlog to done. Work items are represented as cards that move through the workflow as capacity allows, with a focus on limiting WIP to maintain flow and minimize bottlenecks.

91.**Question:** What are the benefits of using Scrum for project management?

Answer: Some benefits of using Scrum for project management include increased transparency and visibility into the project's progress, faster time-to-market through iterative delivery of value, improved collaboration and communication among team members and stakeholders, better adaptability to changing requirements and priorities, and a focus on continuous improvement through regular retrospectives and feedback loops.

92. Question: What are the key roles in Scrum, and what are their responsibilities?

Answer: The key roles in Scrum are the Product Owner, Scrum Master, and Development Team. The Product Owner is responsible for defining and prioritizing the product backlog, representing the stakeholders' interests, and ensuring the team delivers value. The Scrum Master serves as a servant-leader for the team, facilitating the Scrum process, removing impediments, and coaching the team on Agile principles and practices. The Development Team is responsible for delivering the product increment and is self-organizing, cross-functional, and accountable for achieving the sprint goal.

93. Question: How does Scrum promote transparency, inspection, and adaptation?

Answer: Scrum promotes transparency by making all aspects of the project visible to stakeholders through artifacts such as the product backlog, sprint backlog, and burndown charts. Regular ceremonies like sprint planning, daily stand-ups, sprint reviews, and retrospectives facilitate inspection and adaptation. These ceremonies provide opportunities for the team to reflect on their progress, gather feedback, and make adjustments to improve their process and deliver greater value to customers.

94. Question: Have you ever managed a project that required adapting to new technology or tools? How did you ensure a smooth transition for the team?

Answer: Yes, managing projects that involve new technology or tools requires careful planning and coordination. In one project, we transitioned to a new project management software to improve collaboration and efficiency. To ensure a smooth transition, I provided training and support to team members to familiarize them with the new tools and processes. We also conducted pilot tests and feedback sessions to identify any issues or areas for improvement before rolling out the new software to the entire team. By involving team members in the transition process and providing ongoing support, we were able to minimize disruptions and ensure a successful adoption of the new technology.

95. Question: What is the purpose of a sprint review in Scrum?

Answer: The purpose of a sprint review is to inspect and adapt the product increment delivered during the sprint. It provides stakeholders with an opportunity to see the completed work, provide feedback, and suggest changes or improvements. The sprint review enables collaboration between the development team and stakeholders, fosters transparency, and helps ensure that the product meets the stakeholders' needs and expectations.

96. Question: How does Scrum handle changing requirements and priorities?

Answer: Scrum embraces change and flexibility, allowing for evolving requirements and priorities. The product backlog serves as a dynamic list of items, with the Product Owner responsible for prioritizing and refining it based on feedback and changing business needs. Sprint planning meetings provide an opportunity to select and adapt the work for the upcoming sprint based on the current priorities. The iterative nature of Scrum, with short, time-boxed sprints, enables teams to respond quickly to changes and deliver incremental value.

97. Question: How does Kanban differ from Scrum, and when might you choose one over the other?

Answer: Kanban is an Agile methodology focused on visualizing work, limiting work in progress (WIP), and optimizing flow. Unlike Scrum, which operates in fixed-length sprints with predefined roles and ceremonies, Kanban is more flexible and continuous. It allows teams to visualize their workflow on a Kanban board, with columns representing different stages of the process, from backlog to done. Work items are represented as cards that move through the workflow as capacity allows, with a focus on limiting WIP to maintain flow and minimize bottlenecks. Kanban is suitable for teams with unpredictable workloads or where frequent reprioritization is necessary, as it provides real-time visibility into the status of work and enables teams to adapt quickly to changing priorities. Scrum, on the other hand, may be preferred for projects with well-defined goals and a stable team, as its structured framework provides clear roles, ceremonies, and cadence for delivering value iteratively. Ultimately, the choice between Scrum and Kanban depends on the specific needs and context of the project and team.

98.Question: What are some common Scrum ceremonies, and what purpose do they serve?

Answer: Scrum ceremonies are essential rituals that help teams effectively plan, execute, and review their work within the framework. These ceremonies include sprint planning, daily stand-ups, sprint reviews, and sprint retrospectives. Sprint planning occurs at the beginning of each sprint and involves the Product Owner and Development Team collaborating to select items from the product backlog for inclusion in the sprint backlog. The purpose of sprint planning is to define the sprint goal and identify the tasks necessary to achieve it. Daily stand-ups are short, time-boxed meetings held every day to synchronize the team's activities, discuss progress, and identify any impediments or challenges. The sprint review takes place at the end of the sprint and involves the team showcasing the completed work to stakeholders and gathering feedback. The purpose of the sprint review is to validate the work done and gather insights for future iterations. Finally, the sprint retrospective occurs after the sprint review and involves the team reflecting on their process, discussing what went well, what could be improved, and identifying actionable items for the next sprint. Each ceremony serves a specific purpose in the Scrum framework, promoting collaboration, transparency, and continuous improvement.

99.Question: Can you explain the roles and responsibilities within a Scrum team?

Answer: In a Scrum team, there are three primary roles: the Product Owner, Scrum Master, and Development Team. The Product Owner is responsible for representing the interests of the stakeholders, defining the product vision, and maintaining the product backlog—a prioritized list of requirements and features. They collaborate with stakeholders to ensure that the product backlog is aligned with business objectives and customer needs. The Scrum Master serves as a servant-leader for the team, facilitating the Scrum process, removing impediments, and fostering a culture of continuous improvement. They coach the team on Agile principles and practices, ensure adherence to Scrum ceremonies, and shield the team from external distractions. The Development Team consists of cross-functional members who collaborate to deliver the product increment. They are self-organizing and responsible for deciding how to achieve the sprint goal, with a focus on delivering high-quality work that meets the Definition of Done.

100. **Question:** What is Scrum, and how does it differ from traditional project management approaches?

Answer: Scrum is an Agile framework designed to help teams deliver high-value products iteratively and incrementally while adapting to change. Unlike traditional project management approaches that rely on extensive upfront planning and rigid processes, Scrum embraces uncertainty and change. It focuses on delivering value to customers early and frequently, prioritizing collaboration, and fostering a culture of continuous improvement. Scrum achieves this through its iterative development cycles called sprints, typically lasting 2-4 weeks, where teams deliver potentially shippable increments of the product. By breaking down complex projects into manageable chunks, Scrum enables teams to respond to feedback and changing requirements more effectively, resulting in greater customer satisfaction and higher-quality outcomes.

101. **Question:** Can you share an example of a project where you had to manage risks effectively to ensure project success?

Answer: Managing risks effectively is essential for project success. In one project, we identified several potential risks early in the planning phase, including technical challenges, resource constraints, and regulatory changes. To mitigate these risks, I worked closely with the project team to develop risk mitigation strategies and contingency plans. We also established regular risk review meetings to monitor and update our risk register, and we proactively communicated with stakeholders to keep them informed of potential risks and our mitigation efforts. By taking a proactive approach to risk management, we were able to successfully navigate the challenges and deliver the project on time and within budget.

102. Question: Describe your experience with project scheduling and timeline management, including techniques for managing project schedules and resolving scheduling conflicts.

Answer: Project scheduling and timeline management involve developing realistic schedules, monitoring progress, and resolving conflicts to ensure project milestones are met. I utilize techniques such as critical path analysis, Gantt charts, and milestone tracking to create and manage project schedules effectively. In case of scheduling conflicts, I prioritize tasks based on their criticality, negotiate resource allocations, and adjust timelines as needed to maintain project momentum and meet deadlines.

103. Question: Can you discuss your experience with project risk management, including risk identification, assessment, and mitigation strategies?

Answer: Risk management is integral to project success, and I employ a systematic approach to identify, assess, and mitigate potential risks throughout the project lifecycle. I conduct risk identification workshops, utilize risk registers to document identified risks, and assess their impact and likelihood using qualitative and quantitative methods. Mitigation strategies may include risk avoidance, risk transfer, risk reduction, or risk acceptance, depending on the nature and severity of the risk. Regular monitoring and proactive risk management help us anticipate and address potential obstacles, ensuring project success.

104. Question: How do you ensure effective communication and collaboration among geographically dispersed project teams or stakeholders?

Answer: Effective communication and collaboration among geographically dispersed teams or stakeholders require leveraging technology, establishing clear communication channels, and fostering a culture of transparency and inclusion. I utilize video conferencing, collaboration tools, and virtual project management platforms to facilitate real-time communication, document sharing, and collaboration. Regular team meetings, status updates, and project dashboards keep stakeholders informed and engaged, fostering a sense of cohesion and alignment despite physical distance.

105. Question: How do you handle stakeholder resistance or skepticism towards project initiatives, and how do you build stakeholder buy-in and support?

Answer: Stakeholder resistance or skepticism towards project initiatives can pose challenges to project success. I address these concerns by fostering open communication, actively listening to stakeholders' perspectives, and addressing their concerns proactively. By demonstrating the benefits and value of the project, engaging stakeholders in decision-making, and soliciting their input and feedback, I build trust and credibility, fostering stakeholder buy-in and support for project initiatives.

106. Question: How does Agile project management facilitate risk management compared to traditional project management approaches?

Answer: Agile project management facilitates risk management by embracing uncertainty, encouraging early and frequent feedback, and enabling teams to adapt quickly to changing conditions. In traditional project management, risk management often involves extensive upfront planning, risk analysis, and mitigation strategies, which can be time-consuming and may not always address emerging risks effectively. In Agile project management, risks are managed iteratively and incrementally, with teams identifying and addressing potential risks as they arise during the project lifecycle. Agile methodologies like Scrum, Kanban, and Extreme Programming (XP) promote transparency, collaboration, and continuous improvement, allowing teams to identify, assess, and respond to risks in a timely manner, reducing the impact and likelihood of negative outcomes.

107. Question: How does the Agile concept of "working in iterations" contribute to project management practices?

Answer: The Agile concept of "working in iterations" contributes to project management practices by enabling teams to deliver value incrementally, gather feedback early and often, and adapt their plans based on real-world experiences. Working in iterations allows teams to break down complex projects into manageable chunks, prioritize features based on customer value, and deliver working software or products at regular intervals. This iterative approach reduces risk, improves predictability, and accelerates time to market by allowing teams to validate assumptions, learn from failures, and make course corrections as needed. By embracing a cycle of planning, executing, reviewing, and adapting, Agile teams can respond more effectively to changing requirements, market conditions, and stakeholder needs, ultimately delivering better outcomes for their customers and stakeholders.

108.Question: Can you describe a time when you had to lead a project team through a period of uncertainty or change? How did you keep the team motivated and focused?

Answer: Leading a project team through uncertainty or change requires effective communication and strong leadership. In one project, we experienced significant changes in project scope midway through the project, which impacted the team's morale and motivation. To address this, I held regular team meetings to provide updates and address any concerns or questions the team had. I also emphasized the importance of staying flexible and adaptable in the face of change, and I encouraged team members to share their ideas and suggestions for navigating the challenges ahead. By fostering a supportive and collaborative environment, we were able to keep the team motivated and focused on achieving our project goals despite the uncertainty.

109.Question: How does the concept of "self-organizing teams" in Agile project management empower teams to achieve their goals?

Answer: The concept of "self-organizing teams" in Agile project management empowers teams to achieve their goals by giving them autonomy, ownership, and accountability over their work. Self-organizing teams are cross-functional groups of individuals who collaborate closely to deliver value incrementally, without direct supervision or micromanagement. These teams are empowered to make decisions, solve problems, and adapt their plans based on changing conditions, allowing them to respond quickly to customer needs and market dynamics. By fostering a culture of trust, collaboration, and continuous improvement, self-organizing teams can unleash their creativity, innovation, and collective intelligence, leading to higher levels of engagement, productivity, and satisfaction among team members, and ultimately, better outcomes for the project.

110.Question: How does Agile project management promote transparency and visibility in project progress?

Answer: Agile project management promotes transparency and visibility in project progress through practices like daily stand-up meetings, sprint planning sessions, and regular demonstrations of working software or products. These practices provide stakeholders with real-time insight into the team's progress, priorities, and challenges, enabling them to make informed decisions and provide timely feedback. Agile methodologies like Scrum, Kanban, and Extreme Programming (XP) also use visual tools such as kanban boards, burn-down charts, and task boards to make work and workflow visible to all team members and stakeholders, fostering a shared understanding of project status and objectives. By promoting transparency and visibility, Agile project management helps build trust, collaboration, and accountability among team members and stakeholders, driving better outcomes and higher levels of satisfaction for all involved.

111.**Question:** How does the Agile principle of "responding to change over following a plan" influence project management practices?

Answer: The Agile principle of "responding to change over following a plan" influences project management practices by emphasizing flexibility, adaptability, and responsiveness in the face of uncertainty and change. Unlike traditional project management approaches that rely on detailed upfront planning and strict adherence to a predefined plan, Agile methodologies like Scrum, Kanban, and Lean UX embrace change as a natural and inevitable part of the project lifecycle. Agile teams prioritize delivering value early and often, gathering feedback from customers and stakeholders, and adapting their plans based on emerging requirements, market conditions, and technological advancements. By focusing on outcomes rather than outputs and continuously seeking opportunities to improve, Agile project management enables teams to deliver better products, faster, and with greater customer satisfaction.

112.**Question:** How do Agile methodologies like Scrum, Kanban, and Lean UX facilitate stakeholder engagement and collaboration?

Answer: Agile methodologies like Scrum, Kanban, and Lean UX facilitate stakeholder engagement and collaboration by providing opportunities for frequent communication, feedback, and collaboration throughout the project lifecycle. In Scrum, stakeholders are actively involved in the sprint planning, review, and retrospective meetings, where they provide input on priorities, review progress, and provide feedback on deliverables. In Kanban, stakeholders have visibility into the team's workflow and can provide input and feedback on work items as they progress through the system. In Lean UX, stakeholders participate in collaborative design sessions, user research, and prototyping activities, where they contribute their insights and expertise to inform design decisions and validate assumptions. By involving stakeholders early and often, Agile methodologies ensure that their needs and expectations are addressed, leading to higher levels of satisfaction and buy-in for the project outcomes.

113.Question: Can you share an example of a project where you successfully managed stakeholder expectations, even when faced with challenging constraints?

Answer: Managing stakeholder expectations is a critical aspect of project management. In one project, we faced tight deadlines and limited resources, which made it challenging to meet all of our stakeholders' expectations. To manage this, I conducted thorough stakeholder analysis to understand their needs and concerns, and I prioritized their requirements based on their level of importance to the project's success. I also communicated regularly with stakeholders to keep them informed of our progress and manage their expectations, providing realistic timelines and setting clear expectations for what could be achieved within the project constraints. By proactively addressing concerns and managing expectations, we were able to successfully deliver the project on time and within budget, while still meeting our stakeholders' needs.

114.Question: How does the Agile principle of "delivering working software or products frequently" impact project management practices?

Answer: The Agile principle of "delivering working software or products frequently" impacts project management practices by promoting incremental delivery, early validation, and continuous feedback. Unlike traditional project management approaches that prioritize delivering a fully complete product at the end of the project, Agile methodologies like Scrum, Kanban, and Lean UX emphasize delivering value early and often, in small, manageable increments. This allows teams to validate assumptions, gather feedback from customers and stakeholders, and make course corrections as needed, reducing the risk of costly mistakes and ensuring that the final product meets user needs and expectations. By delivering working software or products frequently, Agile project management practices enable teams to demonstrate progress, build trust with stakeholders, and course-correct early, ultimately leading to faster time to market and higher levels of customer satisfaction.

115.Question: How does the Agile concept of "customer collaboration over contract negotiation" influence project management practices?

Answer: The Agile concept of "customer collaboration over contract negotiation" influences project management practices by emphasizing the importance of active engagement, communication, and collaboration between the development team and the customer throughout the project lifecycle. Unlike traditional project management approaches that rely on detailed upfront requirements and fixed contracts, Agile methodologies like Scrum, Kanban, and Lean UX encourage ongoing dialogue and collaboration with customers and stakeholders, enabling teams to respond quickly to changing requirements, priorities, and market conditions. By involving customers early and often, Agile project management practices ensure that their needs and expectations are understood and addressed, leading to higher levels of satisfaction and alignment with the final product. Additionally, by prioritizing collaboration over contract negotiation, Agile teams can focus on delivering value and building long-term relationships with their customers, rather than simply fulfilling contractual obligations.

116.Question: Describe a project where you had to manage scope changes requested by stakeholders. How did you evaluate the impact of the changes and ensure they aligned with project objectives?

Answer: In a project where stakeholders requested scope changes midway through the project, I conducted a thorough impact assessment to evaluate the implications of the changes on project objectives, timeline, and budget. I collaborated with stakeholders to understand the rationale behind the changes and the desired outcomes, and I facilitated discussions to identify alternative solutions that would meet their needs while minimizing disruption to the project. I also communicated transparently with the project team about the scope changes and their implications, ensuring alignment and buy-in from all stakeholders. By managing scope changes strategically and proactively, we were able to maintain project momentum and deliver value to the stakeholders.

117. Question: Have you ever managed a project where you had to make difficult decisions that impacted project timelines or resources? How did you approach these decisions and communicate them to stakeholders?

Answer: Yes, in a project with tight deadlines and limited resources, I had to make difficult decisions to reprioritize tasks and reallocate resources to address critical issues. I conducted a thorough impact analysis to assess the potential consequences of different courses of action and consulted with key stakeholders to solicit their input and feedback. I then communicated the rationale behind the decisions transparently and proactively, highlighting the potential risks and benefits of each option. By involving stakeholders in the decision-making process and providing clear and consistent communication, we were able to navigate the challenges effectively and maintain project momentum.

118. Can you share an example of a project where you had to manage stakeholder expectations during a crisis situation? How did you maintain stakeholder confidence and trust in the project's success?

Answer: In a project facing unforeseen challenges, such as a critical system outage, I maintained open and transparent communication with stakeholders to keep them informed of the situation and our mitigation efforts. I provided regular updates on the progress of resolving the issue and reassured stakeholders of our commitment to delivering the project successfully. I also collaborated with key stakeholders to identify alternative solutions and mitigate any potential impact on project timelines and deliverables. By demonstrating proactive problem-solving and maintaining a focus on stakeholder needs, we were able to maintain stakeholder confidence and trust in the project's success despite the crisis situation.

119. Question: Can you share an example of a project where you had to lead a diverse team with members from different backgrounds and skill sets? How did you foster collaboration and synergy within the team?

Answer: In a recent project, I managed a team consisting of members from various departments and disciplines. To foster collaboration, I organized team-building activities and workshops to help team members get to know each other better and understand each other's strengths and expertise. I also established clear communication channels and encouraged open dialogue to ensure that everyone felt heard and valued. By promoting a culture of inclusivity and teamwork, we were able to leverage the diverse skills and perspectives of the team members to achieve our project goals effectively.

120.**Question:** Have you ever had to manage a project with limited resources? How did you optimize resource allocation to ensure project success?

Answer: Yes, in a previous project, we had budget constraints that required careful resource management. I conducted a thorough analysis of project requirements and team capabilities to identify areas where we could streamline processes and maximize efficiency. We also leveraged technology tools to automate repetitive tasks and minimize manual effort. By optimizing resource allocation and prioritizing tasks based on their impact on project objectives, we were able to deliver the project within budget and meet stakeholder expectations.

121.**Question:** Can you describe a project where you faced significant challenges in meeting deadlines? How did you handle the situation?

Answer: In one project, we encountered unexpected delays due to technical issues with a vendor's software. To address this, I convened an emergency meeting with the project team and stakeholders to reassess our timeline and identify potential solutions. We decided to allocate additional resources to resolve the technical issues and implemented a revised project plan with more realistic deadlines. By proactively addressing the challenges and adjusting our approach, we were able to meet the project deadlines without compromising on quality.

122.**Question:** Have you ever managed a project that required adapting to new technology or tools? How did you ensure a smooth transition for the team?

Answer: Yes, managing projects that involve new technology or tools requires careful planning and coordination. In one project, we transitioned to a new project management software to improve collaboration and efficiency. To ensure a smooth transition, I provided training and support to team members to familiarize them with the new tools and processes. We also conducted pilot tests and feedback sessions to identify any issues or areas for improvement before rolling out the new software to the entire team. By involving team members in the transition process and providing ongoing support, we were able to minimize disruptions and ensure a successful adoption of the new technology.

123.Question: How does the Agile principle of "simplicity" apply to Scrum, Kanban, Lean UX, and Extreme Programming (XP)?

Answer: The Agile principle of "simplicity" applies to Scrum, Kanban, Lean UX, and Extreme Programming (XP) by emphasizing the importance of minimizing complexity, reducing waste, and delivering value incrementally. In Scrum, simplicity is achieved through the use of time-boxed iterations, clear roles and responsibilities, and a focus on delivering the most valuable features first. In Kanban, simplicity is achieved through visual management, limiting work in progress (WIP), and optimizing flow, reducing unnecessary complexity and enabling teams to deliver value more quickly. In Lean UX, simplicity is achieved through rapid iteration, experimentation, and user feedback, ensuring that designs and products are streamlined and intuitive. In Extreme Programming (XP), simplicity is achieved through practices like Test-Driven Development (TDD), Pair Programming, and Continuous Integration, which help teams focus on delivering working software that meets customer needs with minimal overhead and complexity.

124.Question: Have you ever had to manage a project with tight deadlines and limited resources? How did you approach it?

Answer: Yes, I've encountered situations where I had to deliver a project under tight deadlines and with limited resources. One example was when we were tasked with launching a new product feature to coincide with a major industry event. To meet the deadline, I adopted Agile project management principles and prioritized the most critical tasks, focusing on delivering incremental value while managing risk. I also collaborated closely with the team to identify and address any bottlenecks or dependencies, and I leveraged external resources and partnerships to augment our internal capabilities. Through effective communication, resourceful problem-solving, and a collaborative team effort, we successfully delivered the project on time and met our objectives.

125. Question: How does the concept of "timeboxing" in Scrum and "cadence" in Kanban contribute to Agile project management practices?

Answer: Timeboxing in Scrum and cadence in Kanban contribute to Agile project management practices by providing a predictable rhythm and structure to the work process. In Scrum, timeboxing is used to define fixed-length iterations, known as sprints, during which teams plan, execute, and review their work. This creates a sense of urgency and focus, encourages teams to deliver incremental value, and enables stakeholders to predict when features will be delivered. In Kanban, cadence refers to the regular intervals at which work is reviewed, planned, and delivered. By establishing a cadence for activities such as stand-up meetings, backlog refinement, and release planning, teams can synchronize their efforts, maintain momentum, and ensure a steady flow of value to customers.

126. Question: How does Extreme Programming (XP) promote team collaboration and communication?

Answer: Extreme Programming (XP) promotes team collaboration and communication through practices such as Pair Programming, Continuous Integration, Collective Code Ownership, and On-Site Customer. Pair Programming encourages developers to work together at one computer, collaborating on writing code, reviewing each other's work, and sharing knowledge, resulting in higher-quality code and improved team communication. Continuous Integration involves frequently integrating code changes into a shared repository and running automated tests, ensuring that the team remains synchronized and aligned. Collective Code Ownership encourages all team members to take ownership of the codebase, contribute to its improvement, and review each other's code, fostering collaboration and shared responsibility. On-Site Customer ensures that customer representatives are actively involved in the development process, providing feedback, clarifying requirements, and making decisions, helping teams stay focused on delivering value to customers.

127. Question: What is Extreme Programming (XP), and what are its core practices?

Answer: Extreme Programming (XP) is an Agile software development methodology that emphasizes values such as simplicity, feedback, communication, and courage. XP consists of several core practices, including Test-Driven Development (TDD), Pair Programming, Continuous Integration, Collective Code Ownership, and On-Site Customer. TDD involves writing tests before writing code, ensuring that the code meets the desired functionality and is thoroughly tested. Pair Programming involves two developers working together at one computer, collaborating on writing code, reviewing each other's work, and sharing knowledge. Continuous Integration involves frequently integrating code changes into a shared repository and running automated tests to detect and fix integration issues early. Collective Code Ownership encourages all team members to take ownership of the codebase, contribute to its improvement, and review each other's code. On-Site Customer involves having a dedicated customer representative available to the team to provide feedback, clarify requirements, and make decisions.

128. Question: How does Lean UX foster collaboration between designers, developers, and stakeholders?

Answer: Lean UX fosters collaboration between designers, developers, and stakeholders by breaking down silos and encouraging cross-functional teams to work together closely throughout the design process. Rather than working in isolation or passing deliverables back and forth, team members collaborate from the outset, co-creating solutions, sharing ideas, and aligning on goals and priorities. Techniques such as collaborative sketching, design studios, and cross-functional workshops enable teams to generate ideas together, iterate rapidly, and make decisions collaboratively. By involving stakeholders early and often in the design process, Lean UX ensures that everyone has a voice and contributes to creating products and experiences that meet user needs and business objectives.

129. Question: What is Lean UX, and how does it differ from traditional UX design approaches?

Answer: Lean UX is an Agile approach to user experience design that focuses on delivering value to users quickly and iteratively. Unlike traditional UX design approaches, which may involve extensive upfront research, documentation, and design deliverables, Lean UX emphasizes experimentation, collaboration, and learning through rapid iterations. It encourages cross-functional teams to work together closely, breaking down silos between designers, developers, and stakeholders, and validating assumptions through user feedback and real-world testing. Lean UX prioritizes outcomes over output, favoring actionable insights and validated learning over comprehensive documentation.

130. Question: What are the core principles of Kanban?

Answer: The core principles of Kanban include visualizing work, limiting work in progress, managing flow, making policies explicit, and continuously improving. By visualizing work on a Kanban board, teams gain transparency into their workflow and can identify bottlenecks and inefficiencies. Limiting WIP helps prevent overloading the team and maintains a steady flow of work. Managing flow involves optimizing the movement of work items through the workflow to minimize cycle time and maximize throughput. Making policies explicit ensures that everyone understands how work is prioritized, executed, and completed. Continuous improvement encourages teams to reflect on their process regularly and make incremental changes to improve efficiency and effectiveness.

131. Question: How does Kanban help teams manage their work more effectively?

Answer: Kanban helps teams manage their work more effectively by providing real-time visibility into the status of work and enabling teams to optimize their flow. The Kanban board visualizes the workflow, making it easy to see where work is flowing smoothly and where bottlenecks may be occurring. Limiting WIP helps prevent overloading the team and ensures that work is completed before new items are started, reducing multitasking, and improving overall efficiency. Kanban also encourages continuous improvement by identifying opportunities to streamline processes and eliminate waste.

132. Question: How do you manage changes to project scope, schedule, or budget, and what impact do change management processes have on project success?

Answer: Managing changes to project scope, schedule, or budget involves implementing formal change management processes that ensure changes are evaluated, approved, and implemented in a controlled manner. I begin by documenting change requests and assessing their impact on project objectives, deliverables, and constraints. I then review change requests with project stakeholders and sponsor to determine their feasibility, urgency, and alignment with project goals. Approved changes are incorporated into project plans and communicated to relevant stakeholders to ensure everyone is aware of the changes and their implications. By implementing rigorous change management processes, I minimize the risk of scope creep, schedule delays, or budget overruns and maintain project control and accountability throughout the project lifecycle.

133. Question: How do you handle project changes requested by stakeholders mid-project, and what impact do these changes typically have on project scope, schedule, and budget?

Answer: Handling project changes requested by stakeholders' mid-project requires careful evaluation of their impact on project scope, schedule, and budget. I begin by documenting change requests and conducting a thorough impact analysis to assess their implications on project objectives and constraints. I communicate transparently with stakeholders about the potential consequences of the proposed changes, including any adjustments to project scope, schedule, or budget that may be required. If changes are approved, I update project plans and documentation accordingly, ensuring that all stakeholders are informed and aligned with the revised project parameters. By managing project changes effectively, I minimize disruptions and ensure that project objectives are achieved within constraints.

134. Question: Can you discuss your experience with project resource management?
Answer: Resource management is critical for optimizing project performance, and I have extensive experience managing project resources, including human resources, materials, and equipment. This involves

identifying resource requirements, allocating resources effectively to support project objectives, and tracking resource utilization throughout the project lifecycle. I also work closely with resource managers and team leads to ensure that resources are available as needed and address any resource constraints or shortages proactively to minimize their impact on project delivery.

135.Question: How does Scrum handle changing requirements and priorities?

Answer: Scrum embraces change and flexibility, allowing for evolving requirements and priorities. The product backlog serves as a dynamic list of items, with the Product Owner responsible for prioritizing and refining it based on feedback and changing business needs. Sprint planning meetings provide an opportunity to select and adapt the work for the upcoming sprint based on the current priorities. The iterative nature of Scrum, with short, time-boxed sprints, enables teams to respond quickly to changes and deliver incremental value.

136.Question: Can you explain the key differences between Agile and Waterfall methodologies?

Answer: Agile and Waterfall are two distinct project management methodologies. Waterfall follows a linear, sequential approach, where each phase of the project (such as requirements, design, development, testing, and deployment) is completed sequentially before moving to the next phase. In contrast, Agile is an iterative and incremental approach, where the project is divided into small, manageable iterations or sprints. Agile emphasizes flexibility, adaptability, and collaboration, allowing for frequent feedback and adjustments throughout the project lifecycle.

137.Question: How does the planning process differ between Agile and Waterfall methodologies?

Answer: In Waterfall, planning is typically done upfront at the beginning of the project, and the project requirements are documented in detail in a project plan. The entire project is planned and executed based on this initial plan, with minimal room for changes once development begins. In contrast, Agile planning is iterative and adaptive. Agile teams plan and prioritize work for each iteration or sprint based on customer feedback and changing requirements. Planning in Agile occurs continuously throughout the project lifecycle, allowing for flexibility and responsiveness to changing priorities and stakeholder needs.

138. Question: How do Agile and Waterfall methodologies handle project scope changes?

Answer: In Waterfall, project scope is defined upfront during the planning phase, and any changes to the scope are typically addressed through change control processes. Changes to project scope in Waterfall often require formal approval and may impact project timelines and budgets. In Agile, project scope changes are expected and embraced. Agile teams welcome change and prioritize flexibility and adaptability. Changes to project scope can be accommodated easily within Agile through iterative planning, frequent feedback, and incremental delivery of value.

139. Question: How do Agile and Waterfall methodologies manage project risks?

Answer: In Waterfall, risk management is typically addressed upfront during the planning phase, and risk mitigation strategies are implemented to minimize potential risks throughout the project lifecycle. Risks are identified and assessed early, and contingency plans are developed to address potential issues. In Agile, risk management is ongoing and integrated into the project's iterative and incremental approach. Agile teams identify and assess risks continuously throughout the project, adapting their plans and strategies as needed to mitigate risks and maximize project success.

140. Question: How do Agile and Waterfall methodologies handle project documentation?

Answer: In Waterfall, comprehensive project documentation is typically created upfront during the planning phase and maintained throughout the project lifecycle. Documentation includes detailed project plans, requirements specifications, design documents, test plans, and other artifacts. In Agile, documentation is leaner and more flexible. Agile teams prioritize working software over comprehensive documentation, focusing on delivering value to customers quickly. Documentation in

Agile is minimal and typically includes user stories, acceptance criteria, and other artifacts that support the delivery of working software.

www.ingramcontent.com/pod-product-compliance
Lightning Source LLC
Chambersburg PA
CBHW070419230526
45471CB00006B/2884